Critical Thi Detective™

Vocabulary

Book 1

Critical Thinking Detective™ products available in print or eBook form.

Beginning • Book 1 • Book 2
Math Beginning • Math
Vocabulary Book 1 • Vocabulary Book 2

Written by
Diane Hartsig

Edited by
Patricia Gray

Graphic Design by
Scott Slyter

THE CRITICAL THINKING CO.™
www.CriticalThinking.com
Phone: 800-458-4849 • Fax: 541-756-1758
1991 Sherman Ave., Suite 200 • North Bend • OR 97459
ISBN 978-1-60144-940-5

Printed in China by Shanghai Chenxi Printing Co., Ltd. (Apr. 2022)

Table of Contents

About This Book 1
How to Solve These Cases 1
The Antique Double-Dealer 2
The Stray Accomplice 4
The Pilfering Toady 6
The Ring Coveter 8
The Acrid Saboteur 10
The Contrary Instigator 12
The Brazen Bilker 14
The Cogent Denigrator 16
The Disgruntled Defacer 18
The Unencumbered Employee 20
The Wandering Wayfarer 22
The Cunning Customer 24
Answers 26

About the Author

Diane Hartsig earned a journalism degree from Michigan State University and an elementary education degree from Western Michigan University. She has nine years of teaching experience and is currently a fifth-grade teacher. Diane is passionate about promoting children's acquisition and usage of language. She is the author of *Critical Thinking Detective™ - Vocabulary*, *Book 1* and *Book 2* and *Vocabulary Riddles – A-Z Catastrophes, Book 1* and *Book 2*. She lives in Dowagiac, Michigan, with her husband and has three children.

About This Book

Vocabulary is a key component of this collection of fun mysteries for Grades 5-12+. The vocabulary in this book was gathered from a multitude of sources including SAT/ACT word lists and the author's reading selections. The *Merriam-Webster.com Dictionary* provided many of the vocabulary details including usage, look-up popularity, synonyms, and antonyms.

Each activity features between 16 and 25 vocabulary words and every one of them has the potential to implicate or exonerate a suspect. Solving the mysteries requires the reader to evaluate vocabulary words and to analyze and synthesize pieces of information. Critical thinking improves as students assess evidence found through reading comprehension and deductive and inductive thinking skills.

After solving each case, the second part of the activity gives versatility to the vocabulary words as students practice using them in a different context. Readers choose the appropriate word from the word list to complete each sentence. When the word lists contain synonyms, students have flexibility in their choices.

These activities and their vocabulary words are not easy, but don't despair. If you take the time to decipher the unknown words and reread, you'll have sharper critical thinking skills and an expanded vocabulary.

How to Solve These Cases

- Read each activity carefully and keep in mind that all statements are true.
- Each activity establishes two to three parameters to identify the culprit. Consider the parameters as you evaluate the statements from the suspects and witnesses. Drawing a picture is helpful.
- Remember that every vocabulary word is important to solve each case. Consult a dictionary as needed for definitions and pronunciations.
- As you look up words, be aware which are synonyms and antonyms of each other.
- Make notes when you find evidence. Synthesizing more than one piece of evidence can often establish innocence or guilt.
- Use the process of elimination to narrow down each list of suspects.

Read the case below to find evidence to identify the innocent and guilty suspects. Remember, the story and suspects' statements are true.

The Antique Double-Dealer

[1]On Wednesday, October 18 of this year, police from the city of Martinsville received a call about the Martinsville Market. [2]According to its owner, the market consists of multiple vendors with their own booths. [3]Lately the owner has heard customer complaints about a vendor who is foisting lackluster facsimiles at exorbitant prices on credulous customers.

[4]When police arrived, they took the statements below from customers conversant with antiques. [5]After listening to their statements, police arrested one of the four vendors below who later confessed.

Customer Statements

Beverly Cooke: [6]"This was my first time at the market. [7]I have heard discrepant customer reviews, so I wanted to check out all of the vendors. [8]I only spent a few minutes in a senescent dealer's booth, but it was enough to see spurious antiques and hear specious claims."

Lauren Radcliffe: [9]"I shopped for more than an hour and only bought something from the last vendor I visited. [10]The vendor wore a madras shirt and gave veritable, but superfluous details about everything I looked at. [11]I really loved his tenable pricing, but only purchased a brass lamp I couldn't live without."

Miriam Jackson: [12]"I know and say hello to all of the vendors in the market. [13]Whenever I bring someone new to shop with me, I point out the vendor in the puce colored shirt. [14]He speculates in ersatz antiques."

Emily Parlance: [15]"I'm familiar with the vendor in the cyan colored shirt. [16]He has steadfast customers and an irreproachable repute. [17]Last week, while we were chatting, he gave cogent validation of the suspect, who is of tantamount age."

Suspect A

Suspect B

Suspect C

Suspect D

Based on the evidence, circle the suspect who is the Antique Double-Dealer.

After solving the case, write the best vocabulary word to complete each sentence. Each word can only be used once.

cogent	lackluster	tantamount	exorbitant	spurious
irreproachable	superfluous	discrepant	senescent	veritable
steadfast	credulous	puce	validation	
conversant	madras	tenable	foist	

1. Before I pick up my order, I need ______________________ of delivery.
2. I wanted the basic contract without ______________________ add-ons.
3. General education classes make students ______________________ in many areas.
4. The lawyer argued the ______________________ points in the case.
5. The ______________________ addition threw off the mid-century modern aesthetic.
6. I exchanged the purchase for a ______________________ replacement.
7. The sale made the ______________________ price of the item more appealing.
8. The politician relied on ______________________ supporters during the crisis.
9. The nonfiction book was a collection of strange but ______________________ stories.
10. The ______________________ worker preferred a part-time schedule.
11. ______________________ sources contributed to the inaccuracies in the student's report.
12. The scandal tarnished the lawyer's ______________________ reputation.
13. The distracted actor delivered a ______________________ performance.
14. In an unregulated market, fake gems can be ______________________ as real jewels.
15. For my new shirt, I wanted a patterned fabric like ______________________.

Read the case below to find evidence to identify the innocent and guilty suspects. Remember, the story and suspects' statements are true.

The Stray Accomplice

[1]On June 15, Cheboygan Police returned to the Northern Store to finish an investigation started the day before. [2]During their initial visit, police interviewed the store's employees who witnessed a theft of fishing gear. [3]The investigation led to the arrest—and confession—of a suspect. [4]As police gathered more details, the idea of an accessory to the crime became palpable and their search for an at-large accomplice began in earnest.

[5]The staff espied the accomplice conniving with the thief in front of the store before the theft. [6]They walked into the store together and then their paths diverged. [7]During the theft, the accomplice acted as a diversion by addling staff with rambling, vacuous questions and clamoring for items housed in the back of the store.

[8]Police narrowed the suspects to the four shown below. [9]After further questions, one of them confessed to being an accessory and returned the stolen fishing gear.

Alex Hollowman

[10]"I guess I looked suspicious when I walked methodically and sinuously through the store, but I was looking for some unwonted gear. [11]I only interacted with a nescient employee."

Charlie Evans

[12]"I palavered with a friend in front of the store, but we didn't enter concurrently. [13]I know my constant questions vexed the employees."

Andrew Clements

[14]"I overheard John Mather's and a friend's machinations in front of the store. [15]Once inside, I found the employees too sedulous to bother."

John Mather

[16]"My questions flummoxed the employees. [17]They made otiose attempts to attain the things I required."

Based on the evidence, circle the suspect who is the Stray Accomplice.

After solving the case, write the best vocabulary word to complete each sentence. Each word can only be used once.

addle	flummox	sinuously	diverge	diversion
espy	sedulous	connive	otiose	palpable
palaver	concurrent	nescient	vacuous	vex
clamor	machination	unwonted		

1. After the argument, the tension in the air became ______________________.
2. Some video games are educational but most are ______________________ distractions.
3. The spoiled child ______________________ for a treat until the parent relented.
4. Your ______________________ protests will not change the decision.
5. The old acquaintances stopped their shopping to ______________________.
6. I strode confidently toward my destination until the path ______________________.
7. Mosquitos and gnats ______________________ us during our camping trip.
8. The contract's legal jargon ______________________ the client.
9. The driver traveled ______________________ down the mountain.
10. The ______________________ parent attended to the toddler's needs.
11. I ______________________ the quarrel while I was eating lunch in the cafeteria.
12. The children manipulated the ______________________ babysitter.
13. The collaborators met in secret to form their ______________________.
14. My cousin attends a neighboring school, but we have ______________________ vacations.
15. Mainstream galleries spurned the artist's ______________________ creations.

Read the case below to find evidence to identify the innocent and guilty suspects. Remember, the story and suspects' statements are true.

The Pilfering Toady

[1]On September 7, the owner of Frasier's Finery called police to investigate the pilfering of money from the store over several months. [2]The owner was distraught over the theft, because she valued her employees and boasted a low employee turnover.

[3]According to the owner, the store's four managers were the only employees with unfettered access to the money. [4]Several employees witnessed the thieving and described the pilfering manager as the owner's toady. [5]They noted the duplicitousness of the sycophant. [6]The manager routinely superseded adulation for excoriation in the owner's absence.

[7]Police interviewed four employees about their managers. [8]Based on their statements, police arrested one of the suspects. [9]Her subsequent confession appalled the owner.

Employee #1: [10]"June Emery is a long-term employee and the owner's lackey. [11]When the owner is away, June only gasconades about her position."

Employee #2: [12]"To finagle a raise, Eliza Riley ingratiates herself to the owner, but her behavior is perfidious."

Employee #3: [13]"We often work with just a manager. [14]It is atypical to work with both the manager and the owner. [15]When it does happen, Daphne Keene's behavior is tainted with superciliousness."

Employee #4: [16]"Amelia Nielson is rapt with perfunctory concerns; [17]she has no forbearance for the censure of her better."

Based on the evidence, circle the suspect who is the Pilfering Toady.

After solving the case, write the best vocabulary word to complete each sentence. Each word can only be used once.

adulation	gasconade	supersede	duplicitousness	finagle
forbearance	superciliousness	dote	perfunctory	rapt
subsequent	censure	perfidy	toadies	unfettered
appall	ingratiate	sycophants		

1. ______________________ editions of the book addressed its initial mistakes.

2. Teaching someone to drive requires tremendous ______________________.

3. The grandparents took every opportunity to ______________________ on their grandchildren.

4. The first part of the training focuses on ______________________ tasks.

5. ______________________ from its leash, the dog ran free in the park.

6. The trusting boss never suspected the thieving employee of ______________________.

7. It takes ______________________ to correct a teacher in front of a class.

8. Strong leaders do not rely on ______________________ who always agree with them.

9. Volunteering for extra work will not ______________________ you to your boss.

10. The curious children listened with ______________________ attentiveness.

11. I rearranged my schedule to ______________________ a vacation.

12. My mother was ______________________ by the state of my messy room.

13. The slide show was an opportunity to ______________________ about the vacation.

14. Newer technology always ______________________ older technology.

15. The celebrity enjoyed the ______________________ from fans.

Read the case below to find evidence to identify the innocent and guilty suspects. Remember, the story and suspects' statements are true.

The Ring Coveter

[1]Today, police from the city of Chesterton arrested one of the suspects below for stealing a ring from Chesterton Cabochon—an upscale jewelry store in the heart of downtown. [2]The theft occurred on Saturday, August 19, between 1 p.m. and 2 p.m. [3]The four women below were the only customers in the store at the time of the crime.

[4]The sales associate remembered showing the ring to Margaret Beech who haughtily looked it over before giving it back to the assistant. [5]The assistant reported hearing a commendatory comment from Janet Johnson as she returned the ring to its display.

[6]Police approached the crime from the sales associate's correct inference; she believed the thief was appreciably covetous of the ring. [7]The customers' comments appear below. [8]After the arrest, one of the suspects confessed and officers recovered the ring from her home.

Margaret Beech

[9]"I noticed the ring because of its outré color. [10]I asked for a closer look because I thought it would complement a necklace I already own. [11]It turned out to be a bauble."

Tess McGowan

[12]"Sue Bevens and I commented to each other about the ring. [13]She looked at it rapaciously, but I was insouciant to the florid design."

Sue Bevens

[14]"I have an eclectic array of jewelry. [15]If I added the ring to my collection, I knew it would be a boffo."

Janet Johnson

[16]"I am a jewelry connoisseur. [17]I was attracted to the ring's au courant color but its execrable quality made it a bête noire."

Based on the evidence, circle the suspect who is the Ring Coveter.

After solving the case, write the best vocabulary word to complete each sentence. Each word can only be used once.

appreciable	connoisseur	bauble	boffo
commendatory	outré	eclectic	florid
insouciant	au courant	bête noire	cabochon
array	covet	execrable	haughty

1. Guests of the exclusive party were too ______________________ to acknowledge the staff.
2. The considerable ______________________ of choices made choosing arduous.
3. The world traveler amassed a/an ______________________ collection of art.
4. The artist composed her work with inlaid ruby and garnet ______________________.
5. The baroque style of the room called for furnishings with ______________________ details.
6. The model's ______________________ look conformed to the latest trends.
7. The discerning ______________________ patronized the city's best restaurants.
8. The envious neighbor ______________________ the grander home next door.
9. The shop offered overpriced tchotchkes and other ______________________ to tourists.
10. The acclaimed play became the director's most celebrated ______________________.
11. The ______________________ student balked at tutoring.
12. Industrious employees enjoy ______________________ bonuses at the company.
13. As the business failed, it became the owner's ______________________.
14. The reviewer's ______________________ comments encouraged the unknown actor.
15. The ______________________ art clashed with the traditional home's décor.

Read the case below to find evidence to identify the innocent and guilty suspects. Remember, the story and suspects' statements are true.

The Acrid Saboteur

[1]On April 5, the owner of Modern Manufacturing called Rochester Police to investigate the sabotage of a production line. [2]The subversion targeted recently acquired automation. [3]Employees debated the acquisition with fervor. [4]Some saw a palliation of their workload, while others feared a forfeiture of their hours.

[5]The incapacitation caused expensive delays, and the owner was eager to find the culprit. [6]Police interviewed several employees. [7]One described the acrid saboteur as a bleater. [8]Another said the culprit manipulated an aberration to her shift schedule. [9]A third said the saboteur's presence became negligible during the crisis precipitated by the sabotage. [10]Police narrowed the suspects to the four employees shown below. [11]After further questioning, police arrested a suspect who eventually confessed.

Morgan Ridley
[12]"I kvetch to accentuate the challenges facing the company. [13]On the night of the sabotage, management repudiated my prowess."

Aimee Tenison
[14]"Rene and I were working our customary, prosaic shifts and carping about the management when the sabotage occurred. [15]My presence became inane after the sabotage."

Rene Autherson
[16]"I have shared my rancor about the company with my co-workers. [17]After the sabotage, the managers did not avail my acumen, which rankled me further."

Emily White
[18]"On the night of the sabotage, management modified Morgan's and my schedule. [19]My dissension didn't preclude me from an impactful effort to restore the impaired production line."

Based on the evidence, circle the suspect who is the Acrid Saboteur.

After solving the case, write the best vocabulary word to complete each sentence. Each word can only be used once.

aberration	forfeiture	rancor	carp	dissent
fervor	prowess	avail	precipitate	preclude
prosaic	acumen	palliate	repudiate	subversion
accentuate	inane	rankle		

1. The yearbook ______________________ the school's successes.
2. The jurors' ______________________ led to a hung jury.
3. The promotion highlighted the long-time employee's ______________________.
4. The committed protestors marched with ______________________.
5. The company negotiated with the union to ______________________ the discord.
6. A large tax increase ______________________ the town's property owners.
7. An authoritarian decree ______________________ the employees' walkout.
8. The teenager's ______________________ increased after the unfair punishment.
9. The donated box was full of useless items the charity could not ______________________.
10. As an employee of the company, you are ______________________ from entering the contest.
11. The convoluted argument was ______________________ to the discussion.
12. After losing the bet, the gambler offered money as ______________________.
13. The unhappy workers plotted their ______________________.
14. The shopper preferred flea markets for their lack of ______________________ items.
15. The overwhelmed worker could not ______________________ the helpful offer.

Read the case below to find evidence to identify the innocent and guilty suspects. Remember, the story and suspects' statements are true.

The Contrary Instigator

[1]Recently, administrators from the Amherst Academy investigated a fray on school grounds. [2]The incident took place at 3:30 p.m. as school was dismissing. [3]Several students were involved and no one was hurt, but the instigator's identity was undetermined. [4]According to witnesses, the melee commenced after the instigator goaded another student with disparaging epithets. [5]The inciter was infamous in the school community for his recalcitrance with superiors and his loquaciousness with peers—especially in class.

[6]Administrators interviewed four students whose statements appear below. [7]After reviewing the statements, school personnel confronted the instigator. [8]He confessed to starting the melee and vowed to amend his contrary ways.

Student #1: [9]"My locker is next to the voluble Trevor Reynolds. [10]In my opinion, he is trying to regale himself with his waywardness and mordant monikers."

Student #2: [11]"Martin Rowen is laconic with his classmates and truculent with authority. [12]He has acute sobriquets for everyone he knows."

Student #3: [13]"Kenny Knuth is my neighbor, and I have known him for a long time. [14]His unsavory conduct is confined to his classmates."

Student #4: [15]"I sit next to Peter Higgins in biology and calculus, and he is quite garrulous. [16]In my experience, he has been deferent with everyone at school."

Trevor Reynolds

Martin Rowen

Kenny Knuth

Peter Higgins

Based on the evidence, circle the suspect who is the Contrary Instigator.

After solving the case, write the best vocabulary word to complete each sentence. Each word can only be used once.

acute	goad	mordant	deferent	loquacious
garrulous	moniker	contrary	laconic	truculent
melee	commence	instigate	regale	
amend	infamous	recalcitrant	fray	

1. There is a process to ______________________ the Constitution of the United States.
2. During the debate, the students offered two ______________________ viewpoints.
3. The student's antics made him ______________________ in the school.
4. It is difficult to interview a ______________________ subject.
5. The ______________________ student won a citizenship award.
6. The court jester ______________________ the royal entourage.
7. The audience waited patiently for the program to ______________________.
8. The bully tried to ______________________ the student with taunts.
9. The ______________________ observer offered a helpful compromise.
10. The bored students tried to ______________________ a food fight.
11. The ______________________ guest talked to everyone at the party.
12. The celebrity adopted her ______________________ as her stage name.
13. The argument escalated into a ______________________.
14. The ______________________ juvenile rebelled against authority.
15. The harsh criticism brimmed with ______________________ commentary.

Read the case below to find evidence to identify the innocent and guilty suspects. Remember, the story and suspects' statements are true.

The Brazen Bilker

[1]On March 7, Buchanan Police investigated the Brazen Bilker, a swindler who duped dilettantish investors of the Buchanan retirement community. [2]The victims—who were conned over several years—represented a wide range of affluence.

[3]The artifice was elementary. [4]The bilker audaciously inflated the worth of chaffy parcels of land and impelled investors to buy them. [5]To feign faculty, the bilker preened in modish attire and fabricated his former achievements.

[6]The police took the statements of four experts with knowledge pertinent to the investigation. [7]Based on the information, police arrested one of the four suspects below. [8]He later confessed and offered restitution to his victims.

Expert #1: [9]"Some of the victims were dubious of their contracts and sought my adjuration. [10]I can corroborate Phillip Laymans and Eric Drummond's temerity during their deals."

Expert #2: [11]"Phillip Layman works exclusively with consummate investors. [12]The others promote a more inclusive clientele."

Expert #3: [13]"I've been an investment advisor for 20 years. [14]Jeff Foust's accomplishments are illustrious in our field."

Expert #4: [15]"Peter Scott and Eric Drummond cultivate land investments. [16]Peter Scott is calculable and candid in his dealings. [17]Eric Drummond's negotiations are clearly more artful."

Peter Scott

Phillip Layman

Jeff Foust

Eric Drummond

Based on the evidence, circle the suspect who is the Brazen Bilker.

After solving the case, write the best vocabulary word to complete each sentence. Each word can only be used once.

adjuration	corroborate	impel	chaffy	calculable
consummate	illustrious	brazen	fabricate	faculty
feign	audacious	dubious	pertinent	preen
artifice	dilettantish	modish		

1. The ______________________ carpenter built the shoddy shelves.
2. The college freshmen utilized the available resources for ______________________.
3. There were several ______________________ achievements in the writer's celebrated career.
4. My conscience ______________________ me to help you with your difficulties.
5. To protect the storyteller's feelings, I ______________________ interest in the narrative.
6. The black tie affair requires guests to ______________________ for the occasion.
7. The once ______________________ house became dated over time.
8. I sifted through the material to identify the ______________________ details.
9. According to the appraiser, my inherited painting is ______________________.
10. The writer provided numerous sources to ______________________ the assertion.
11. I was ______________________ of the plan and hesitated to join it.
12. The department needed the ______________________ of its senior members to run smoothly.
13. I relied on the ______________________ electrician to update the old house's wiring.
14. The ______________________ teenager repeatedly broke curfew.
15. The intricate ______________________ employed several co-conspirators.

Read the case below to find evidence to identify the innocent and guilty suspects. Remember, the story and suspects' statements are true.

The Cogent Denigrator

[1]Recently, Fran's Flower Shop in Bay City experienced an abatement in sales. [2]The decrement confounded the shop's owner, Fran, who has enjoyed robust business and a sterling reputation for the past 15 years. [3]To investigate, Fran surveyed her customers. [4]Several alluded to abysmal reviews of the shop from an indignant former client. [5]According to the scuttlebutt, the discerning client commissioned the shop for a sumptuous event. [6]The meager flower arrangements caused discontentment, and she became a cogent denigrator of the shop to her friends.

[7]Based on the description, Fran narrowed the list of suspects to the four clients shown below. [8]When one of the suspects admitted to the deprecation, Fran offered an amicable resolution to regain the long-time customer.

Ellie Winters

[9]"On the advice of my friends, I contracted Fran's Flowers for my daughter's wedding a few months ago. [10]The ceremony lacked ostentation, with a felicitous amount of flowers."

Helen Kent

[11]"Every year, I throw an opulent party for the holidays. [12]My last party—sans the exiguous centerpieces—was seamless. [13]After the festivities, I made sure to convey my pique to all of my friends."

April Comstock

[14]"A couple of months ago, I solicited Fran's Flowers for my parents' anniversary party. [15]Fran noticed my chagrin over the paltry flower arrangements and appeased me by revamping my order. [16]I've extolled her malleability ever since."

Rebecca Owens

[17]"I am well known for hosting lavish events. [18]After every one, I proffer my candid opinion to my friends. [19]Lately I've been lauding Fran's fecundity with floral displays."

Based on the evidence, circle the suspect who is the Cogent Denigrator.

After solving the case, write the best vocabulary word to complete each sentence. Each word can only be used once.

abysmal	exiguous	proffer	candid	decrement
discerning	pique	appease	laud	malleability
opulent	amicable	felicitous	seamless	sumptuous
allude	fecundity	sans		

1. Reviewers ______________________ the artist for his achievement.
2. Both parties benefitted from the ______________________ agreement.
3. The well-designed house appeals to a ______________________ buyer.
4. The student's transition from middle school to high school was ______________________.
5. The lack of rain caused the reservoir's ______________________.
6. I was still hungry after the ______________________ dinner.
7. The move to a new city will test your ______________________.
8. Despite the forecast, I left ______________________ umbrella.
9. The inventor's ______________________ led to many breakthroughs.
10. The therapist's calming words ______________________ the anxious patient.
11. The palatial home boasts ______________________ interiors.
12. I offered my ______________________ opinion after reading the book.
13. The restaurant's ______________________ reviews hastened its closure.
14. The snub from the awards show heightened the actor's ______________________.
15. The volunteer ______________________ her help without reservation.

Read the case below to find evidence to identify the innocent and guilty suspects. Remember, the story and suspects' statements are true.

The Disgruntled Defacer

[1]Today Saginaw Police arrested one of the four suspects shown below for vandalizing a company sign at Innovative Technology. [2]A construction worker temporarily placed the sign near the employee lounge at 2 p.m. [3]He reported the sign's damage two hours later when he retrieved it for installation.

[4]The company's manager explained the high turnover at the company. [5]He correctly inferred the defacer was a disgruntled employee and was most cynical about an inept subordinate. [6]Police interviewed four employees who utilized the lounge during the time in question. [7]After the arrest, one of the suspects confessed.

The Suspects

Kyle Liffkin
[8]"I would be more adroit if I could forge a more prudent position in the company. [9]I have worked for Innovative Technology for an aggrieved year. [10]My co-workers and I are in consensus about the predicaments involved with our jobs. [11]In fact, Henry Hartsig and I often condole each other."

James Eastwood
[12]"Innovative Technology has stringent policies, but I've been auspicious since joining the company six months ago. [13]The day can be arduous when I work with feckless co-workers such as Austin Anders and Kyle Liffkin."

Henry Hartsig
[14]"The manager can be capricious, but overall, this job has been ameliorating for me. [15]I know who the vandal is, and I believe dogged chastisement fomented him."

Austin Anders
[16]"As a fledgling employee, I have made innumerable mistakes. [17]The manager has always been commiserative of my callowness. [18]I have seen him reproach Kyle Liffkin and James Eastwood—the former for fallacious reasons—many times."

Based on the evidence, circle the suspect who is the Disgruntled Defacer.

After solving the case, write the best vocabulary word to complete each sentence. Each word can only be used once.

adroit	chastisement	inept	auspicious	callowness
capricious	foment	arduous	fallacious	feckless
fledgling	ameliorating	dogged	reproach	stringent
aggrieve	consensus	innumerable		

1. The supervisor fired the ______________________ employee for a multitude of mistakes.
2. The parents relented after the child's ______________________ protests.
3. The ______________________ songwriter signed his first contract.
4. A lack of ______________________ stalled the plan's implementation.
5. To move into the building, you must adhere to its ______________________ policies.
6. The opportunistic troublemaker ______________________ the restless crowd.
7. A lack of directions made the assembly more ______________________.
8. The ______________________ family supported several local charities.
9. The teacher ______________________ the student for the disruption of class.
10. There are ______________________ ways to make a difference in your community.
11. The public ______________________ humiliated the worker.
12. The new intern chalked up the mistake to ______________________.
13. To clear my head, I took a/an ______________________ walk in the country.
14. The ______________________ supervisor assigned duties haphazardly.
15. The ______________________ heirs challenged the will in court.

Read the case below to find evidence to identify the innocent and guilty suspects. Remember, the story and suspects' statements are true.

The Unencumbered Employee

1On December 15 of this year, the manager of the Midtown Store called Rogers City Police. 2She explained that an envelope of money she intended to deposit in the bank had disappeared from the store's office while it was unattended on a desk. 3Employees have access to the office—using it to count their till, which is locked in a drawer at the conclusion of their shifts. 4The manager left the office around 10 a.m. to unlock a display case for a customer. 5Upon leaving, she had a headlong encounter with Natalie Derringer. 6When the manager returned fifteen minutes later, the envelope was missing.

7Police interviewed a customer who was the only witness to the crime and four employees who were working at the time of the theft. 8The witness said the crime occurred incontinently after the manager left the office. 9Police used the employees' statements, listed below, to arrest a suspect, who later confessed.

Marian Shaunders
10"When the store opens at 9 a.m., the manager allocates morning assignments. 11I was diligently executing my charges when the envelope vanished. 12I saw the thief. 13She was unencumbered by imperatives."

Vivienne Richards
14"I summoned the manager to open the case. 15During her discourse with the customer, I tarried contiguously about until my aptitude became integral to the purchase."

Natalie Derringer
16"Our manager is peremptory. 17This morning, she relegated me to an elongated list of burdens which I, of course, abrogated."

Lizzie Rathmore
18"I circumvented the manager and most of my co-workers during the foremost part of my shift. 19Marian Shaunders was the only exception; she vainly asked if I could facilitate her onus."

Based on the evidence, circle the suspect who is the Unencumbered Employee.

After solving the case, write the best vocabulary word to complete each sentence. Each word can only be used once.

abrogate	facilitate	relegate	contiguous	diligent
elongated	peremptory	circumvent	incontinently	integral
onus	aptitude	imperative	unencumbered	vainly
allocate	headlong	tarry		

1. The teacher ______________________ scissors and rulers at the beginning of the year.
2. The children waited until they were alone to ______________________ their chores.
3. The prodigy displayed an early ______________________ for music.
4. Late employees are ______________________ to undesirable tasks.
5. Management passed the ______________________ without consideration of its implications.
6. The executive hired an assistant to ______________________ the workload.
7. The concession stand is ______________________ to the football field.
8. The bill must be paid ______________________ to avoid late fees.
9. The child's ______________________ Christmas list continued to grow.
10. The ______________________ of transporting equipment rested on the band members.
11. Some workers ______________________ after their shifts to socialize with co-workers.
12. Vocabulary is ______________________ to the understanding of geometry.
13. The ______________________ retiree enjoyed the reduction of stress.
14. The housekeeper ______________________ tried to clean the stain.
15. On the playground, no one wanted to play with the ______________________ child.

Read the case below to find evidence to identify the innocent and guilty suspects. Remember, the story and suspects' statements are true.

The Wandering Wayfarer

[1]On April 5, Grand Rapids Police arrived at Paul Bovair's home to investigate an ongoing trespassing of his property. [2]Mr. Bovair, his wife, and three children live on Monroe Street in a home with an expansive yard. [3]He explained that an interloper has been exploiting his yard as a shortcut to the nearby park. [4]Mr. Bovair described the interloper's pace as hastened and said his fence was no deterrence. [5]The lone interloper with invariant behavior infiltrates the yard from the alley behind the home between 3 p.m. and 4 p.m.

[6]Police questioned four suspects who were walking in the alley during the hour in question. [7]After analyzing their statements, and asking one suspect additional questions; police took one suspect into custody; who later confessed.

Clark Bolen

[8]"Rendezvousing with friends at the park is part of my immutable schedule. [9]I'm always short on time, so my brisk constitutional utilizes the most expedient route."

Scott Reagan

[10]"Periodically, I take a stroll to the park, but my path abuts the peripheries of others' properties. [11]I've seen others encroach on private property including Clark Bolen and Don Jerrod who will vault any barrier."

Lewis Stevens

[12]"My schedule includes a walk to the park after class. [13]Today is an anomaly. [14]I usually coalesce with my peers, including Scott Reagan, for the leisurely jaunt."

Don Jerrod

[15]I'm a college senior who's been walking to the park for years. [16]I will forsake communal spaces as a solitary traveler but that happens intermittently. [17]It's more prevalent to be in an assemblage of friends."

Based on the evidence, circle the suspect who is the Wandering Wayfarer.

After solving the case, write the best vocabulary word to complete each sentence. Each word can only be used once.

abut	hastened	periphery	constitutional	deterrence
encroach	invariant	coalesce	immutable	interloper
intermittently	assemblage	infiltrate	rendezvous	wayfarer
anomaly	jaunt	prevalent		

1. The driver used cruise control for a/an ______________________ speed.
2. My job requires me to travel abroad ______________________.
3. Stakes mark the ______________________ of our property.
4. An auditor spotted the ______________________ in the paperwork.
5. After my car broke down, I became a/an ______________________.
6. The ______________________ gained entry by breaking a window.
7. Despite the fence, rabbits and deer still ______________________ my garden.
8. The owner's absence ______________________ the old house's decline.
9. The ______________________ to grandma's house includes a scenic drive.
10. Our backyard ______________________ with our neighbor's yard.
11. It is ______________________ for college freshmen to change their majors.
12. In the summer, I take my ______________________ early, before it becomes too hot.
13. The warring factions ______________________ to fight their common enemy.
14. A/An ______________________ of authors headlined the charity event.
15. The group dispersed but agreed to ______________________ later.

Read the case below to find evidence to identify the innocent and guilty suspects. Remember, the story and suspects' statements are true.

The Cunning Customer

[1]On December 1 of this year, Jennison City Police investigated the theft of a bracelet from Jennison's Fine Jewelry. [2]The bracelet disappeared between 4 p.m. and 5 p.m. from a display on the jewelry counter. [3]Police interviewed four witnesses. [4]The first witness said the thief was not a devout customer of the store. [5]The second witness said the theft transpired while the sales associate heeded a persnickety customer's tirade. [6]A third witness said the sales associate abetted the thief before she attended to the exacting customer.

[7]Police took the statements from the four suspects listed below. [8]After weighing the evidence, police arrested one of the suspects, who later confessed, and police retrieved the bracelet from her possession later that day.

Margaret Mathers

[9]"I was interested in some jewelry but deferred my own questions to the staff until the fastidious customer finished her rant. [10]I saw Helen Speath enter the store amid the harangue."

Helen Speath

[11]"The store is not a haunt of mine. [12]I was looking for a gift and came to the store based on the recommendation of a co-worker. [13]I have no convictions about the harried sales associate who left my queries unresolved."

Anna Knox

[14]"I am a stalwart fixture in the store and recommended it to my friend, Margaret Mathers. [15]Since then, she has become an inveterate patron."

Angela Payne

[16]"I sporadically shop in the store. [17]I found the sales associate to be obliging even though the store was bustling. [18]I can attest to the moiling attention the finicky customer necessitated."

Based on the evidence, circle the suspect who is the Cunning Customer.

After solving the case, write the best vocabulary word to complete each sentence. Each word can only be used once.

abet	harangue	persnickety	devout	exacting
fastidious	query	bustling	inveterate	necessitate
obliging	attest	heed	stalwart	transpire
amid	harried	sporadically		

1. During the summer, the beach is ______________________ with tourists.
2. The ______________________ host provided us with excellent accommodations.
3. The ______________________ fan never misses a basketball game.
4. The collector saw the treasures ______________________ the junk.
5. The impressive trophy ______________________ a custom-built case.
6. Please direct all ______________________ to the information desk.
7. The guide advised the tourists to ______________________ all posted signs.
8. The architect prepared multiple designs for the ______________________ client.
9. ______________________ habits can be difficult to break.
10. Pop-up rain showers happen ______________________ without warning.
11. The loud ______________________ drew stares from bystanders.
12. The clueless substitute unknowingly ______________________ the class troublemaker.
13. After a barrage of questions, the speaker became ______________________.
14. I can ______________________ to the applicant's strong work ethic.
15. The event ______________________ while I was absent.

Answers

The Antique Double-Dealer (pages 2-3)

The Innocent

Suspect A: In sentences 10 and 11, Lauren Radcliffe states that a vendor wearing a madras shirt gives veritable, but superfluous details, but she buys a lamp at a tenable price. This proves Suspect A's innocence.

Suspect C: In sentences 15 and 16, Emily Parlance describes a vendor in a cyan shirt who has steadfast customers and an irreproachable repute. This proves Suspect C's innocence.

Suspect D: In sentence 17, Emily Parlance states that Suspect C gives cogent validation of the suspect vendor, who is Suspect D. Suspect C is young and he is talking about a vendor of tantamount age which could only be Suspect D. This proves Suspect D's innocence.

The Antique Double-Dealer

Suspect B is the Antique Double-Dealer because a process of elimination exonerates the other suspects. In sentence 5, we learn the police arrested one of the four vendors, who confessed. Since we can prove the innocence of Suspects A, C, and D, we know that Suspect B is our double-dealer. In sentence 8, Beverly Cooke's also provides evidence Supporting Suspect B's guilt when she describes a senescent vendor who was selling spurious antiques and making specious claims. He is further implicated by Miriam Jackson's statements in sentences 13 and 14 that a vendor in a puce shirt is speculating ersatz antiques.

1. validation
2. superfluous
3. conversant
4. cogent or tenable
5. discrepant
6. tantamount
7. exorbitant
8. steadfast
9. veritable
10. senescent
11. spurious
12. irreproachable
13. lackluster
14. foisted
15. madras

Vocabulary Words and Appropriate Synonym for Context Within Case

Vocabulary Word	Synonym
cogent	compelling
conversant	knowledgeable
credulous	naive
cyan	greenish blue
discrepant	clashing
ersatz	fake
exorbitant	inflated
foist	pass off
irreproachable	faultless
lackluster	uninspired
madras	striped or checked
puce	dark red or purple brown
senescent	aged
specious	deceptive
spurious	bogus
steadfast	constant
superfluous	extra
tantamount	equivalent
tenable	defendable
validation	confirmation
veritable	authentic

The Stray Accomplice (pages 4-5)

Alex Holloman

Charlie Evans

Andrew Clements

John Mather

The Innocent

Alex Hollowman: In sentence 5, the accomplice connives with the thief. From sentence 11, we know Hollowman only interacted with an employee. This proves Alex Hollowman's innocence.

Charlie Evans: From sentence 6, the thief and accomplice walk into the store together. In sentence 12, Evans entrance to the store is not concurrent with his friend. This proves Charlie Evans' innocence.

Andrew Clements: In sentence 7, the accomplice is acting as a diversion by addling employees with questions. Clements finds the employees too sedulous to bother in sentence 15. This proves Andrew Clements' innocence.

The Stray Accomplice

John Mather is the Stray Accomplice because a process of elimination exonerates the other suspects. From sentence 9, we know police arrested a suspect who confessed to being the accessory. Sentence 5 tells us the accomplice connives with the thief. In sentence 14, Clements overhears the machinations of Mather and a friend. From sentence 7, we know the accomplice acted as a diversion by addling the employees with questions and clamoring for items housed in the back. In sentence 16, Mather says his questions flummoxed employees, and in sentence 17 we learn employees made otiose attempts to attain things he required.

1. palpable
2. vacuous
3. clamored
4. otiose
5. palaver
6. diverged
7. vexed
8. addled or flummoxed
9. sinuously
10. sedulous
11. espied
12. nescient
13. machination
14. concurrent
15. unwonted

Vocabulary Words and Appropriate Synonym for Context Within Case

Vocabulary Word	Synonym
addle	confuse
clamor	demand
concurrent	simultaneous
connive	scheme
diverge	split
espy	observe
flummox	confuse
machination	plot
nescient	clueless
otiose	futile
palpable	unmistakable
palaver	talk
sedulous	engaged
sinuously	windingly
unwonted	unique
vacuous	mindless
vex	bother

The Pilfering Toady (pages 6-7)

June Emery

Eliza Riley

Daphne Keene

Amelia Nielson

The Innocent

June Emery: In sentence 6, the pilferer excoriates the owner in her absence. From sentence 11, we know Emery only gasconades about her position in the owner's absence. This proves June Emery's innocence.

Daphne Keene: In sentence 4, the pilferer is the owner's toady. When Keene is with the owner, superciliousness taints her behavior according to sentence 15. This proves Daphne Keene's innocence.

Amelia Nielson: In sentence 6, the pilferer excoriates the owner in her absence. From sentence 17, we know Nielson has no forbearance for the censure of her better. This proves Amelia Nielson's innocence.

The Pilfering Toady

Eliza Riley is the Pilfering Toady because a process of elimination exonerates the other suspects. From sentences 8 and 9, we know police arrested one of the suspects who subsequently confessed. In sentence 4, the pilferer is the owner's toady. In sentence 12, Riley ingratiates herself to the owner. From sentence 5, we know the pilferer's behavior is duplicitous. In sentence 12, Riley's behavior is perfidious.

1. subsequent
2. forbearance
3. dote
4. perfunctory
5. unfettered
6. duplicitousness or perfidy
7. superciliousness
8. sycophants or toadies
9. ingratiate
10. rapt
11. finagle
12. appalled
13. gasconade
14. supersedes
15. adulation

Vocabulary Words and Appropriate Synonym for Context Within Case

Vocabulary Word	Synonym
adulation	flattery
appall	shock
censure	disapproval
dote	adore
duplicitousness	disloyalty
excoriation	scathing disapproval
finagle	engineer
forbearance	patience
gasconade	brag
ingratiate	brown-nose
lackey	follower
perfidious	disloyal
perfunctory	routine
rapt	absorbed
subsequent	later
superciliousness	arrogance
supersede	set aside
sycophant	suck-up
toady	yes-man
unfettered	free

The Ring Coveter (pages 8-9)

Margaret Beech

Tess McGowan

Sue Bevens

Janet Johnson

The Innocent

Margaret Beech: From sentence 6, we know the thief is appreciably covetous of the ring. In sentence 4, Beech looks at it haughtily. In sentences 9 and 11, Beech calls it a bauble with an outré color. This proves Margaret Beech's innocence.

Tess McGowan: From sentence 6, we know the thief is appreciably covetous of the ring. In sentence 13, McGowan is insouciant, and she calls the ring's design florid. This proves Tess McGowan's innocence.

Janet Johnson: From sentence 6, we know the thief is appreciably covetous of the ring. In sentence 17, Johnson describes the ring's quality as execrable and labels the ring a bête noire. This proves Janet Johnson's innocence.

The Ring Coveter

Sue Bevens is the Ring Coveter because a process of elimination exonerates the other suspects. From sentence 8, we know police arrested one of the suspects. That suspect confessed and police found the ring at her home. In sentence 6, we know the thief is appreciably covetous of the ring. In sentence 13, Bevens looks rapaciously at the ring. In sentence 15, Sue Bevens looks at the ring as a potential addition to her jewelry collection and calls it a boffo.

1. haughty
2. array
3. eclectic
4. cabochons
5. florid
6. au courant
7. connoisseur
8. coveted
9. baubles
10. boffo
11. insouciant
12. appreciable
13. bête noire
14. commendatory
15. outré

Vocabulary Words and Appropriate Synonym for Context Within Case

Vocabulary Word	Synonym
appreciable	detectable
array	variety
au courant	fashionable
bauble	trinket
bête noire	dislikable item
boffo	success
cabochon	polished gem
commendatory	favorable
connoisseur	expert
covet	desire
eclectic	assorted
execrable	awful
florid	excessively decorated
haughty	arrogant
insouciant	disinterested
outré	bizarre
rapacious	greedy

The Acrid Saboteur (pages 10-11)

Morgan Ridley

Aimee Tenison

Rene Autherson

Emily White

The Innocent

Aimee Tenison and **Rene Autherson**: In sentence 8, the saboteur manipulates an aberration in her shift schedule. In sentence 14, Tenison and Autherson are working their customary, prosaic shifts. This proves Aimee Tenison and Rene Autherson's innocence.

Emily White: In sentence 9, the saboteur's presence is negligible during the crisis. In sentence 19, White's dissent does not preclude her from an impactful effort to restore the impaired production line. This proves Emily White's innocence.

The Acrid Saboteur

Morgan Ridley is the Acrid Saboteur because a process of elimination exonerates the other suspects. From sentence 11, we know police arrested one of the suspects who eventually confessed. In sentence 8, the saboteur manipulates an aberration in her shift schedule. In sentence 18, management alters Ridley's schedule. Sentence 7 describes the saboteur as a bleater. In sentence 12, Ridley refers to her kvetching. In sentence 9, the saboteur's presence is negligible during the crisis. From sentence 13, we know management repudiated Ridley's prowess.

1. accentuated
2. dissent
3. acumen or prowess
4. fervor
5. palliate
6. rankled
7. precipitated
8. rancor
9. avail
10. precluded
11. inane
12. forfeiture
13. subversion
14. prosaic
15. repudiate

Vocabulary Words and Appropriate Synonym for Context Within Case

Vocabulary Word	Synonym
aberration	variation
accentuate	highlight
acrid	bitter
acumen	understanding
avail	use
bleat	complain
carp	complain
dissent	disagreement
fervor	passion
forfeiture	loss
inane	insubstantial
kvetch	complain
negligible	inconsequential
palliate	ease
precipitate	cause
preclude	prevent
prosaic	ordinary
prowess	skill
rancor	resentfulness
rankle	anger
repudiate	refuse
subversion	undermining

The Contrary Instigator (pages 12-13)

Trevor Reynolds Martin Rowen Kenny Knuth Peter Higgins

The Innocent

Martin Rowen: In sentence 5, the instigator is loquacious with his peers but in sentence 11, Rowen is laconic with classmates. In addition, the instigator goads with a disparaging epithet in sentence 4. From sentence 12, we know Rowen has acute sobriquets for everyone he knows. This proves Martin Rowen's innocence.

Kenny Knuth: In sentence 5, the instigator is recalcitrant with superiors. From sentence 14, we know Knuth confines his unsavory conduct to his peers. This proves Kenny Knuth's innocence.

Peter Higgins: From sentences 4 and 5, we know the instigator goads classmates and is recalcitrant with his superiors. In sentence 16, Higgins is deferent to everyone in school. This proves Peter Higgins' innocence.

The Contrary Instigator

Trevor Reynolds is the Contrary Instigator because a process of elimination exonerates the other suspects. From sentence 8, we know one of the suspects confessed to being the instigator of the melee. In sentence 5, the instigator is loquacious with his peers. In sentence 9, a student calls him voluble. Sentences 4 and 5 tell us about the instigator's disparaging epithets and recalcitrance. Sentence 10 confirms Reynold's mordant monikers and waywardness.

1. amend
2. contrary
3. infamous
4. laconic
5. deferent
6. regaled
7. commence
8. goad
9. acute
10. instigate
11. garrulous or loquacious
12. moniker
13. fray or melee
14. recalcitrant or truculent
15. mordant

Vocabulary Words and Appropriate Synonym for Context Within Case

Vocabulary Word	Synonym
acute	insightful
amend	change
commence	begin
contrary	opposing
deferent	respectful
disparaging	derogatory
fray	scuffle
epithet	descriptive phrase
garrulous	talkative
goad	provoke
infamous	well known for a bad quality
instigate	start
laconic	using few words
loquacious	talkative
melee	scuffle
moniker	nickname
mordant	biting
recalcitrant	defiance
regale	amuse
sobriquet	nickname
truculent	defiant
unsavory	off-putting
voluble	talkative
waywardness	defiance

The Brazen Bilker (pages 14-15)

Peter Scott

Phillip Layman

Jeff Foust

Eric Drummond

The Innocent

Peter Scott: From sentence 1, we learn the bilker dupes dilettantish investors. In sentence 16, the expert calls Scott calculable and candid. This proves Peter Scott's innocence.

Phillip Layman: In sentence 1, we learn the bilker dupes dilettantish investors. In sentence 11, Layman works exclusively with consummate investors. This proves Phillip Layman's innocence.

Jeff Foust: From sentence 5, we know the bilker feigns faculty and fabricates former achievements. In sentence 14, Foust's accomplishments are described as illustrious. This proves Jeff Foust's innocence.

The Brazen Bilker

Eric Drummond is the Brazen Bilker because a process of elimination exonerates the other suspects. From sentences 7 and 8, we know police arrested one of the suspects who later confessed and offered restitution to his victims. Other supporting evidence includes sentences 1, 17, 4, 10, 15, and 5. In sentence 1 we learn that the bilker dupes investors. In sentence 17, Drummond's negotiations are artful. In sentence 4, the bilker is audacious. In sentence 10, Drummond has temerity. From sentence 4, we know the bilker entails land deals. In sentence 15, Drummond cultivates land investments. In addition, from sentence 5, we know the bilker preened in modish attire.

1. dilettantish
2. adjuration
3. illustrious
4. impelled
5. fabricated or feigned
6. preen
7. modish
8. pertinent
9. chaffy
10. corroborate
11. dubious
12. faculty
13. calculable or consummate
14. audacious or brazen
15. artifice

Vocabulary Words and Appropriate Synonym for Context Within Case

Vocabulary Word	Synonym
adjuration	advising
affluence	wealth
artifice	scheme
artful	cunning
audacious	daring
brazen	bold
bilker	scammer
candid	truthful
chaffy	worthless
calculable	dependable
consummate	experienced
corroborate	confirm
dilettantish	unskilled
dubious	doubtful
fabricate	manufacture
faculty	competence
feign	fake
illustrious	noteworthy
impel	pressure
modish	trendy
pertinent	relevant
preen	dress up
temerity	brashness

The Cogent Denigrator (pages 16-17)

Ellie Winters

Helen Kent

April Comstock

Rebecca Owens

The Innocent

Ellie Winters: In sentences 5 and 6, the denigrator's event is sumptuous with meager flower arrangements. In sentence 10, Winters says her daughter's wedding lacks ostentation and calls the flower arrangements felicitous. This proves Ellie Winters' innocence.

April Comstock: In sentence 4, the denigrator is indignant. In sentence 15, a revamped order appeases Comstock. In sentence 16, Comstock extolls Fran. This proves April Comstock's innocence.

Rebecca Owens: In sentence 4, the denigrator is giving Fran's shop abysmal reviews. In sentence 19, Comstock lauds Fran for her fecundity with floral displays. This proves Rebecca Owens' innocence.

The Cogent Denigrator

Helen Kent is the Cogent Denigrator because a process of elimination exonerates the other suspects. In sentence 8, we know one of the suspects admitted to the denigrator's deprecation. In sentence 5, the denigrator's event is sumptuous. In sentence 11, Kent throws opulent parties. In sentence 6, meager flower arrangements cause the denigrator's discontentment. In sentence 12, Kent's centerpieces are exiguous. In sentence 6, the suspect denigrates the shop to her friends. In sentence 13, Kent conveys her pique to her friends.

1. lauded
2. amicable
3. discerning
4. seamless
5. decrement
6. exiguous
7. malleability
8. sans
9. fecundity
10. appeased
11. opulent or sumptuous
12. candid
13. abysmal
14. pique
15. proffered

Vocabulary Words and Appropriate Synonym for Context Within Case

Vocabulary Word	Synonym
abatement	reduction
abysmal	awful
allude	mention
amicable	agreeable
appease	disarm
candid	honest
cogent	persuasive
confound	confuse
decrement	decrease
denigrate	belittle
discerning	insightful
exiguous	skimpy
fecundity	inventiveness
felicitous	appropriate
indignant	resentful
laud	praise
lavish	elaborate
malleability	adaptability
opulent	elaborate
ostentation	showiness
pique	resentment
proffer	offer
sans	without
seamless	perfect
sumptuous	elaborate

The Disgruntled Defacer (pages 18-19)

Kyle Liffkin

James Eastwood

Henry Hartsig

Austin Anders

The Innocent

James Eastwood: In sentence 5, the manager correctly inferred the defacer was a disgruntled employee. In sentence 12, Eastwood credits the company with making him auspicious. This proves James Eastwood's innocence.

Henry Hartsig: In sentence 5, the manager correctly inferred the defacer was a disgruntled employee. In sentence 14, Hartsig calls his job ameliorating. This proves Henry's Hartsig's innocence.

Austin Anders: In sentence 5, the manager correctly inferred the defacer was a disgruntled employee. In sentence 17, Anders states the manager is commiserative of his innumerable mistakes. This proves Austin Anders' innocence.

The Disgruntled Defacer

Kyle Liffkin is the disgruntled defacer because a process of elimination exonerates the other suspects. From sentences 1 and 7, we know the police arrested one of the suspects who later confessed. In sentence 5, the manager correctly inferred the defacer was a disgruntled employee and is cynical of an inept subordinate. In sentence 9, Liffkin calls his yearlong employment aggrieved. In sentence 13, Eastwood calls Liffkin feckless. In sentence 14, Hartsig identifies the vandal as a doggedly chastised employee. Sentence 18 lists Liffkin as a frequently reproached employee.

1. feckless or inept
2. dogged
3. fledgling
4. consensus
5. stringent
6. fomented
7. arduous
8. auspicious
9. reproached
10. innumerable
11. chastisement
12. callowness
13. ameliorating
14. capricious
15. aggrieved

Vocabulary Words and Appropriate Synonym for Context Within Case

Vocabulary Word	Synonym
adroit	skillful
aggrieved	resentful
ameliorating	beneficial
arduous	difficult
auspicious	prosperous
callowness	immaturity
capricious	inconsistent
chastisement	scolding
consensus	agreement
commiserative	pitying
condole	express sympathy
dogged	persistent
fallacious	mistaken
feckless	incompetent
fledgling	inexperienced
foment	provoke
inept	unsuccessful
innumerable	countless
reproach	to express disapproval
stringent	strict

The Unencumbered Employee (pages 20-21)

Marian Shaunders

Vivienne Richards

Natalie Derringer

Lizzie Rathmore

The Innocent

Marian Shaunders: From sentence 11, we know Shaunders was diligently executing her charges when the envelope vanished. This proves Marian Shaunders' innocence.

Vivienne Richards: In sentence 14, we learn that Richards summoned the manager. Sentence 15 tells us she tarried contiguously about during the manager and customer's discourse until her aptitude became integral to the purchase. In sentence 8, we learn the envelope disappeared incontinently after the manager left the office. This proves Vivienne Richards' innocence.

Natalie Derringer: From sentence 8, we know the theft occurred incontinently after the manager left the office. In sentence 5, we learn about the manager's headlong encounter with Derringer upon leaving the office. This proves Natalie Derringer's innocence.

The Unencumbered Employee

Lizzie Rathmore is the Unencumbered Employee because a process of elimination exonerates the other suspects. From sentence 9, we know the police arrested one of the suspects who later confessed. In sentence 13, we learn the thief is unencumbered by imperatives. From sentence 10, we know the manager allocates morning assignments. Sentence 18 tells us Rathmore circumvented the manager. In addition, from sentence 19, we know Shaunders vainly asks Rathmore to facilitate her onus.

1. allocated
2. abrogate or circumvent
3. aptitude
4. relegated
5. imperative
6. facilitate
7. contiguous
8. headlong or incontinently
9. elongated
10. onus
11. tarry
12. integral
13. unencumbered
14. vainly
15. peremptory

Vocabulary Words and Appropriate Synonym for Context Within Case

Vocabulary Word	Synonym
abrogate	evade
allocate	assign
aptitude	ability
circumvent	bypass
contiguous	bordering
diligent	painstaking
elongated	extended
facilitate	ease
headlong	without pause
imperative	command
incontinently	immediately
integral	necessary
onus	burden
peremptory	bossy
relegate	demote
tarry	linger
unencumbered	unburdened
vainly	producing no result

The Wandering Wayfarer (pages 22-23)

Clark Bolen

Scott Reagan

Lewis Stevens

Don Jerrod

The Innocent

Scott Reagan: In sentence 5, we learn that the trespasser was alone and that he doesn't change his behavior. In sentence 10, we learn that Reagan only goes to the park occasionally. In sentences 13 and 14, Stevens tell us that he usually goes to the park with Reagan, so this proves Scott Reagan's innocence.

Lewis Stevens: In sentence 5, we learn there is only a lone interloper with invariant behavior. In sentences 13 and 14, Stevens said the day was an anomaly because he usually coalesced with his peers for the jaunt. This proves Lewis Stevens' innocence.

Don Jerrod: In sentence 5, we learn there is only a lone interloper with invariant behavior. In sentence 16, Jerrod forsakes communal spaces only intermittently. In sentence 17, Jerrod states it is more prevalent to be in an assemblage of friends. This proves Don Jerrod's innocence.

The Wandering Wayfarer

Clark Bolen is the Wandering Wayfarer because a process of elimination exonerates the other suspects. Sentence 7 tells us that police arrested one of the four suspects and one of them confessed. In sentence 5, we learn there is only one interloper with an invariant pattern. In sentence 8, Bolen is rendezvousing with friends at the park and calling his schedule immutable. In sentence 11, Reagan names Bolen as someone he has seen encroaching on others' property and states he will vault any barrier. In sentence 4, we know the homeowner's fence is no deterrence for the interloper.

1. invariant or immutable
2. intermittently
3. periphery
4. anomaly
5. wayfarer
6. interloper
7. infiltrate
8. hastened
9. jaunt
10. abuts
11. prevalent
12. constitutional
13. coalesced
14. assemblage
15. rendezvous

Vocabulary Words and Appropriate Synonym for Context Within Case

Vocabulary Word	Synonym
abut	border on
anomaly	irregularity
assemblage	group
coalesce	unite
constitutional	walk
deterrence	obstacle
encroach	creep
hastened	hurried
jaunt	pleasurable journey
infiltrate	pass into
immutable	unchanging
interloper	intruder
intermittently	occasionally
invariant	constant
periphery	boundary
prevalent	common
rendezvous	meet
wayfarer	foot traveler

The Cunning Customer (pages 24-25)

Margaret Mathers

Helen Speath

Anna Knox

Angela Payne

The Innocent

Margaret Mathers: In sentence 6, we learn that the third witness saw the thief being assisted by the sales associate before attending to the exacting customer. This is the same customer that is described in sentence 5 as persnickety and launched a tirade just before the theft. In sentence 9, we learn that Mathers deferred to ask a question until the fastidious customer finished her rant. In sentence 4, the first witness states that the thief was not a devout shopper at the store. In sentence 15, Knox calls Mathers an inveterate (habitual) patron. This proves Margaret Mathers' innocence.

Helen Speath: In sentence 10, Mathers states that Speath arrived in the store amid the customer's harangue. In sentence 6, we learn that the third witness saw the thief assisted by the sales associate before attending to the exacting customer. This is the same customer that is described in sentence 5 as persnickety and launched a tirade just before the theft. This proves Speath's innocence since she arrived in the store during the tirade.

Anna Knox: In sentence 4, the first witness states that the thief was not a devout shopper at the store. In sentence 14, Knox states that she is a stalwart fixture in the store. This proves Anna Knox's innocence.

The Cunning Customer

Angela Payne is the Cunning Customer because a process of elimination exonerates the other suspects. Sentence 8 tells us that the police arrested one of the four suspects and one confessed. In sentence 4, the first witness states that the thief was not a devout shopper at the store. In sentences 16 and 17, Payne states she is a sporadic shopper in the store and that an obliging sales associate waited on her. In addition, in sentence 18 she attested to the moiling attention the finicky customer necessitated.

1. bustling
2. obliging
3. devout or stalwart
4. amid
5. necessitated
6. queries
7. heed
8. exacting, fastidious, or persnickety
9. inveterate
10. sporadically
11. harangue
12. abetted
13. harried
14. attest
15. transpired

Vocabulary Words and Appropriate Synonym for Context Within Case

Vocabulary Word	Synonym
abet	help
amid	among
attest	vouch
bustling	busy
devout	faithful
exacting	particular
fastidious	choosy
finicky	picky
harangue	rant
harried	strained
heed	regard
inveterate	deep-rooted
moiling	difficult
necessitate	need
obliging	accommodating
persnickety	fussy
query	question
sporadically	occasionally
stalwart	reliable
transpire	occur